Poems, Parkinson's, And The Things That Inspire Me

Hywel Griffiths QPM

A further collection of poems
written from the heart.

Bwyddfa Ccmisiynydd
Yr Heddlu a Throseddu
GWENT
Office of Police and
Crime Commissioner

In aid of
PARKINSON'SUK
CHANGE ATTITUDES.
FIND A CURE.
JOIN US.

Thanks and Acknowledgements:

My personal and very good photographer
Mr Robert Morgans.

My dedicated team of loyal and dedicated typists:

Karen GIFFORD
Alison REYNOLDS
Sarah GRIFFITHS
Emma ISAAC
Debbie MITSON

This collection of poems has been written:

- As a tribute to the courage and spirit shown by the daughter of a work colleague, in the face of a serious illness. Young Daisy should be seen as an outstanding example of the human spirit and the determination to succeed that many of us should aspire to. Daisy – You truly are an inspiration.
- As a tribute to the wonderful and selfless contribution to music made by the members of the heroic Military Wives Choirs & the inspirational Gareth MALLONE

It also contains:

- poems written in remembrance by me for members of the armed forces and the civilian police who have been willing to sacrifice all – even their lives in protection of our freedoms and our values.
- some poems which reflect the level of my support and appreciation for the Royal Family.
- Other poems about my personal battles in my war with Parkinson's disease, and:
- The benefits of living life with an optimistic and positive attitude – and by wearing a smile on your face.
- Anything else that made me smile and/ or inspired me!

Hywel GRIFFITHS QPM

The Poems

Daisy

A Daisy really is a magical flower,
It can brighten up even the darkest of days most dour,
And I know of one very special girl with the same name,
And the positive effect she has is exactly the same.

Because it really does upset me; it makes me quite sad,
But the more that I think of it – it actually makes me quite mad;
And what makes me mad are those people who have the gall,
To moan about everything - when their grievances are so trivial and small!

So I think we should ignore them – not even give them a mention,
And rather praise those like young daisy who deserve all the attention.
Because for those who face adversity with courage and a smile,
I will endeavour to do my best for them – and go that extra mile!

It's not just because of the illness which Daisy must face each day,
But it's the positive way she deals with it which is why I feel that I must say:
Daisy – you truly are an inspiration to everyone including me
And the joy you bring to those whose hearts you touch
is plain there for all to see!

The Military Wives Choirs

To honour those willing to give of their lives,
And those who support both husbands and wives,
I've taken five minutes to express how I feel;
For people to realise that my feelings are real.

'Home they brought her warrior dead'
Emotionally powerful - even when read,
Feelings stripped bare, nerve endings raw,
Facing the fact - your partners are at war.

With great humility I write you these rhymes
With great respect I try and capture the times,
Helped greatly by Gareth, who'll go to any length,
To help you to cope, to help give you strength.

I speak for the country - You have the support of us all
so walk tall with pride and with pride walk tall,
And like the story told by the magical warhorse,
you too can be strong - you too can be a force.

Because the songs you sing about your partners abroad,
Are all emotionally strong, and will strike an emotional cord.
To commemorate the century of World War One,
You can congratulate yourself on a job well done

Military (Husbands) and Wives

A tribute not asked for,
A tribute not planned,
I just want to say Thank You,
To those who fight for our land.

Whether in the Armed Forces,
Or in the Police,
Much work unknown,
Not for public release.

Yet the servants of The Queen,
Are willing to lay down their lives,
To protect all of our freedoms,
Our families; husbands and wives.

All that I ask for,
And nothing else would I expect,
Just think of them daily,
They've earned our total respect.

The Inspirational Gareth Malone

"Who inspires you most?" asked a poll on TV.
Well I thought to myself "Just who might that be?"
I suppose if asked to choose by myself all alone,
It would surely be the conductor Mr Gareth MALONE.

So just who is this Gareth and why make him first choice?
Well he can make a random collection sing as if with one voice.
Most recently he made famous those great army wives,
Showing what can be done if you take control of your lives.

Alas for myself I am unable to sing,
And I can never experience the joy this must bring,
But I am not alone as I have an identical twin brother,
And to be honest when we sing we're as bad as each other!

Now our mother dear could sing so clear,
You could say that she really did have a passion,
But if you heard her sing – without any fear,
You'd know her style of singing had gone totally out of fashion!

To finish this poem – we begin again at the begin,
And give praise and thanks to the man who makes those choirs sing.
Gareth you have thanks and gratitude, not just from me on my own,
Because we'd all like to praise the inspirational Gareth MALONE!

Those Games Called INVICTUS

I openly talk about having Parkinson's disease,
And how I overcome it apparently with ease,
And though I sometimes moan and have a little grumble,
What I've witnessed today makes me feel ever so humble.

I watched some competitors at those games called 'Invictus',
Where the courage displayed should inspire every one of us,
Because watching these athletes, oft with no arms, legs or sight,
Has made me look at myself and ask "How bad is my plight".

These courageous young people from Her Majesty's Forces,
Now compete on the track rather than tackling assault courses,
One person stands out and our words we should not mince,
The burden of success was largely borne by Harry - Our Prince.

What these games show is the healing power of sport,
And what can be achieved if given the right support,
And if for their sacrifices we can give these people a new start,
Then it is a cause that we should support with all of our hearts.

They would walk 500 miles

Great is my admiration for the Military Wives,
Supporting our Forces who regularly risk their lives,
Often their contribution is not recognised at all'
Long lonely hours hoping they never get the call.

So many of our soldiers, sailors and airmen injured in wars,
Doing so willingly because they are committed to the cause,
The cause is freedom and security, a cause that is right and is just,
The fate of our nation put into strong hands that we can trust.

The partners of our troops who are always there for support,
Providing a service that simply couldn't be bought,
Have found a unique way of getting together in support of 'Our Boys'
They've formed themselves into choirs that make lots of noise!

I personally have no doubt that they would walk at least 500 miles,
And I'm sure at the end of the day they'd still be talking – full of
laughter and smiles,
The least we can do to help them do their duty and still have some fun,
Is to buy their new record and make sure it's a Christmas number one.

GOOD LUCK LADIES
RESPECT

We would walk 500 miles

When we wake up, well, we know we're gonna be,
We're gonna be the choir who sings out for the boys.
When we go out, yeah, we know we're gonna be,
We're gonna be the choir who makes the loudest noise!

If we get drunk, well, we know we're gonna be.
We're gonna be the choir who gets drunk on the punch;
And if we're thrown out, we know we're gonna be
We're gonna be the first choir to start the party after lunch!

Because we are those famous military wives,
Who support our troops and brighten up their lives?
And much more joy we will soon be bringing
As we release our song with all us girls singing:

Na –Ne – Na - Na.
Na –Ne – Na - Na.
Na –Ne – Na - Na.
Na –Na – Na – Ne
Na –Ne – Ne - Na.- Ne.

Trouble

(It's the Name of the Game)

Some think it's funny,
It's all part of the game,
To single people out,
Simply because of a name.

But then society itself,
Does exactly the same,
Using labels of identity,
To name and to shame.

Identity is an issue,
Vital to modern day life,
Prejudice and ignorance,
Fuelled where gossip is rife.

Identity is what defines us,
Enabling us to form into groups,
Like joining a football club,
Or fighting for the Queen's Troops.

And this concept of forming groups –
Willing to help one another,
Should be fostered and nurtured,
Friends or foe seen like sister or brother.

And we may have a future free from strife and from wars;
If we wake up to the fact that we're all fighting for the same cause.

Retired But Refired

The time has come for me to retire,
Put on my slippers and sit in front of the fire,
But I'm not the sort just to sit in front of a telly,
I've got too much to do – too much fire in my belly.

A fire that burns to help a good cause,
A fire that burns for those who fight all our wars,
Young people who fight for us and give up their lives,
There are none so supportive as the military wives.

These fantastic people up of country wide groups,
Are there for each other, as well as supporting our troops,
And I will do anything and whatever is in my power,
To raise the profile of these people who never wilt – never cower.

But there is one thing I can't do which you may find strange,
I can't hit any note – whatever the range;
But I'm still glad to support you as you support our boys,
By forming your choirs – and making lots of noise!

Ghosties and Ghoulies

Skeletons in the cupboard,
Monsters in the bed,
Ghosts and ghouls are all around,
It's the kingdom of the dead.

Werewolves out and stalking,
Vampires looking for new blood,
And down at the deep dark lagoon,
You'll find those 'creatures made from mud'

King Kong is on the rampage,
Godzilla has eaten the odd school bus or two,
We're now searching for a hero to rescue us
And of course - only the best will do!

And that hero walks amongst us;
Appearing all powerful and oh so strong;
The only one who can save the day is my mother-in-law
Wearing killer curlers and a thong!!!!

My Parkinson's Nurse

(The Remarkable Debbie DAVIES)

My Parkinson's Nurse has been like an angel to me,
Helping me to cope – encouraging me to be the best I can be.
Giving me strength, at my side she has always been there,
Through times both good and then bad with the same level of care.

From initial devastation where everything seemed so bleak;
When I couldn't see past the next day never mind the next week.
But Debbie my nurse convinced me that together we could cope,
As long as I believed and didn't give up my hope.

And that in short is the story of my life,
Not giving enough credit to people like Debbie or my wife.
Because although people see how Parkinson's affects me,
They often overlook the fact that it doesn't just affect me.

So I'd like to take a moment to thank each and every one of you,
Who have helped and encouraged me in all I have tried to do.
And the results and successes that I have achieved,
Would not have been possible if you had not all believed...

Believed that Parkinson's would have no dominion over me;
Believed I would fulfil my promise to 'Be the Best that I can Be!'

A Poetic Farewell

I've got to say it, though some may call it a sin,
It gives me great pleasure to sit on top of a washer at fast spin.
And after that start which I know will upset my wife,
I'll just take two minutes to give a breakdown of my life.

It won't take me long - I promise to keep it short,
A boy from the valleys – Rugby Union the sport.
Close friends, close family – I won't go too deep.
But I mustn't forget about those pretty mountain sheep.

Got a job with the police and caught a few crooks,
Wrote a couple of poems which I had published in books,
Then without even asking – not even saying please,
I've had to share my life with Parkinson's disease.

It's not always easy, though my troubles I try to hide,
The disease is insidious it eats away at you from the inside.
And whatever doubts or criticisms you may have about me.
You can't argue with the fact I always try to be the best I can be.

And so with the help and support of you all,
You've helped me to keep my pride and walk tall,
Then with a smile on my face and by showing how I cope,
My legacy is a symbol of optimism and hope!

KEEP SMILING

A Fond Farewell from a Friend

After 31years of loyally serving the Queen,
I'd like to look back on what a journey it's been,
Dreaming at one point of becoming a great detective,
I designed a new role as Gwent's Greatest Defective.

Firstly, I'd like to say "I'm humbled and thank-you to each one and all".
Your support has enabled me to carry on and with pride to walk tall.
But time waits for no-one – not even Gwent's very own bard;
Who would ever believe that writing this poem would be so hard?

With my life-long companion of Parkinson's disease,
I've shown how much easier life is if you smile and say 'Please'.
One thing they promised me about this Parkinson's curse;
It's a degenerative condition that can only get worse.

But cheer up be happy don't let this get you down,
I try to live my life happy – never to consider a frown.
If there's one thing I'd like you all to remember from me:
How I face each new day by striving to be the best I can be.

I have lived for the job for my whole working life,
And now is the time to pay more attention to my wife.
She has always been there for me like the Rock of Gibraltar,
Always at my side - never once did she waiver or falter.

Throughout my service there's been no hidden agenda or aim,
I've tried to help other others – spurred on by the flame:
The flame that lights the fires burning so deep down inside,
To show those who commit crime - they have nowhere to hide.

I bid farewell to you all –
And as the work up high it keeps piling,
Just spare a thought for me,
And for my sake,
KEEP SMILING

A whole lot of MACCA

One's a Macca,
Two's a Macca
Hit the ground –
Apparently there's a whole lot of
Macca that's a going round and round!

Schumacca,
BlueMaccca,
Poops in a stream,
Are they all our memories –
Or just part of Macca's dream –
Though the way old Macca's smiling –
He looks like the cat who's had the cream!

Good days –
Happy days –
Days we never will forget,
Not when you recall some characters;
Good old fluffy Durham and the one and only Brett!
Days we lived together through our teenage years,
Our recent get to-gethers blowing away the fears,
Now we have friendships that with trust go hand-in-hand,
The bonds that form these friendships –
Only we will understand!

Three A-Macca,
Two A-Macca;
There is only one true Macca,
And I'm glad to call him a friend!

The Power of Song

Hot News from the Press,
Our boys need help from the stress,
so they've turned to our fabulous guru,
Singing her heart out for the troops,
This lady would jump through flaming hoops,
Who else could it be but the remarkable LULU.

...and I have very little doubt,
That to support them she will shout;
And sing from the rafters don't CRY;
As our forces must be focussed and true,
Ready to counter what our enemies might do
And in this they often face a real life do-or-die.

So it is no wonder that many of our troops suffer,
As they fight to maintain an indestructible buffer,
Often hiding the terror and trauma that they feel.
The Military Wives Choirs help them to stay strong,
Is by using the healing powers and comfort of song,
To support our troops in their mental battles so real.

Me and My Parkie

Wobbling, Staggering – unsteady on my feet,
It's just me walking to the sound of the Parkinson's beat.
Stared at – laughed at and now really comes rub,
If I go for a drink – the bouncers follow me around the pub!

And though I laugh about it and try to have a joke,
Eventually this ridicule would affect the most insensitive of folk.
And sometimes you hear the voices of people talking quietly out loud,
Pointed comments and derision that really shouldn't be allowed.

And why some people do it I still can't work out fully,
But what they do is even worse than the actions of an old school bully;
And just like a bully, these people will seek, the vulnerable and frail,
Which is why we must ensure that their ignorance shall never prevail.

Because one thing I know about this Parkinson's curse,
As a degenerative illness my walking can only get worse.
...and so I would ask you, all of my relatives and friends,
To help in my aim to see that this ignorance and mockery ends.

Because hidden within, is someone who really does care,
That person is me and I'm becoming increasingly self-aware!

Cry

Cry,
Cry
Why, cry?
Why, Why, Indeed?

Cry,
Cry,
Why high?
Why high, the need?

Cry,
Cry,
Cry tears,
From leaky eyes they speed!

Cry,
Cry,
Shout out,
Shout out cry to lead.

Cry,
Cry,
Cry Gently
Cry enough they plead.
try to put them in order,
Cry for their wives with their inten#ons so pure,
Cry for those who just pray for a cure.

In Praise of Volunteers

I've just taken five minutes to write this little rhyme,
In praise of those special people willing to give up their time!
They do this quite gladly because they are people who care,
And at any time you need them – they will always be there.

These volunteers are vital to our service – The National Health,
They contribute because they want to – not because of the Wealth!
And perhaps special praise should go to those quite often unsung;
These people often criticised are those volunteers who are young.

What they do should not just be recognised by their generation,
But should be lauded and celebrated by the whole of the Nation.
They should be seen as an example, and as role models for all,
And my message to them, is to stand proud and stand tall.

Then my message to all you very special volunteers,
Enjoy being in the limelight and we'll raise up some cheers,
To give you recognition and praise, which is so richly deserved,
For those volunteers who ensure that we are so well served.

Thank You – Diolch!

Parkinson's awareness week

18TH-24TH April 2016

What have I said,
What have I done,
Why does everyone laugh,
Why do they always make fun?

Is it because of my wonkety walk,
Or even maybe it's my lopsided run,
Or is it because of my quick quiet voice;
That they always seem to make fun?

I don't think they've given it a thought,
Or even taken some time for a little think,
How it feels when you can't walk in a straight line
The classic test to see if you've had a drink!

Because even if I seem to be lost,
In my own little private place,
I'm still fully aware of all that goes on,
Even if I wear a mask upon my face!

So please be aware and give some thought,
The reason for this rhyme,
That hidden by all of the symptoms,
Is a sufferer with Parkinson's;
...who just needs a little time.

Baz do this

Baz do this,
And Baz do that,
Baz did go to college;
To learn how to dead do a rat.

Then Baz did this,
And Baz did that,
There would be no need to do either,
If he just did buy a cat

But it's not just rats
That digs them holes,
You've got moles, voles,
And them cats called poles.
And last of all but they are the best,
Are those pirates who dig holes
...to fill with their chest!

And what a to do would all that cause!

Bad Santa

Santa's on a diet

(An alternative look at Christmas)

Santa's on a diet
He's too big for his sleigh,
Rudolph would have a hernia,
Not good for Christmas Day!

The other reindeer backed him,
Saying we're going a strike
"But what about that bike for Jimmy
Or his sister's little trike"

The Fairy said we can't have this,
It's the season of good will,
And the perfect present for Santa
Is a magic dietary pill.

Well this is the story that Santa gave,
When at Crown Court he did plead
To grooming some young reindeer
And flying high on Speed!

But Santa got no sympathy,
From his enemies or from his mates;
He only works one night all year,
And then claims Bank Holiday rates.

From Up North to the Beautiful South

Way back in the middle of the eighties,
Were some of the happiest days of my life.
Lads used to play and bathe with their Mateys –
And it was the time I first met my beautiful wife.

My beloved was brought up in a house,
In North Wales - on the Costa Del Scouse,
Close to the thriving Metropolis of Rhyl,
She knew me before I joined the Old Bill!

And now as my career nears the end,
I'm proud that my wife is still my best friend,
As when I asked her if she would be my wife,
It was the best decision I ever made in my life.

I'd like to ask you to thank Karen for the last 30 years,
Full of memories of both laughter and tears,
And if you ask why I love and respect you so much,
If I was the Sweeney, she was my Gentle Touch,

And coming to see your concert tonight,
Fills us both full of expectation and delight,
if I mistime my tablets I'll look like I'm frozen to the core,
But if I get it right – I'll be the best god-damn break-dancer,
...on that concert floor.

ALL THANKS TO PARKINSON 'S DISEASE

My Poetry and Me

If asked to describe my poetry – where would I start
Well, I know that all of my poems come straight from the heart.
But I don't mean romance, love poems or that sort of thing,
I refer to poems that inspiration and hope they can bring.

Many of my poems refer to my battle with Parkinson's disease,
And my refusal to let this condition bring me down onto my knees.
It's not easy, but I get on with it – I'm just that sort of guy,
And my main line of defence is to never let myself wonder why.

Another common theme or so goes the rumour,
Is that most of them aim to have a little bit of humour.
Of course with my breakdancing and cute little wiggle,
That in itself is enough to make anyone giggle.

But people can look and decide for themselves,
By buying my book which will soon be on the shelves,
Called 'Poems, Parkinson's, the Police and Me',
It shows how I cope by trying to be the 'Best I can Be'

The 'Legend' That is: Martin Jones

Martin – we have known each other for many long years,
With many stories and tales – most of which nearly bring me to tears.
We've tackled burglars and thieves and crooks of all sort,
Not many have we missed – but many more have we caught.

One tale you tell is of a memorable night in Ebbw Vale,
When an attempt to burgle a house was destined to fail.
And in fairness to you on that cold fateful old night,
You stayed late on the scene until my dog had his bite.

But it's after this that the real story does start,
When we find out what happened to the wife of 'our Mart'.
Because as Martin worked on, he didn't seem to care,
She got hypothermia – waiting alone in cold bleak Aberdare.

And then we move onto the famous Operation 'Scupper'
Where a major crime gang met their maker in Ebbw Vale Upper,
Caught by a group of maverick cops, each one a great detective,
Led by Mr SUTTON with assistance from me – the PC defective.

Your finest moment was when you squared up to Sonny,
A champion bare knuckle boxer who didn't mean to be funny
When he said 'I'm the hardest man in Britain, what you got?'
Martin replied 'It's me from Merthyr and on that last point, you're not'

Then as these two squared up like a violent barn dance,
Willie, instructed by Mr SUTTON took his one and only chance,
And with his unique and risqué form of Irish smarm,
He talked two giants out of doing each other some harm.

Martin I could go on writing letter by letter,
And like you the stories would get better and better.
But even the best story must finish, and I'll say at the end –
Martin, I'm proud and honoured to call you a friend.

Wishing you a long and happy retirement, Hywel

A poem for two Special People

This poem is written for two special people today,
As they both take their vows, and "I Do" they do say.
And what they must realise now they are husband and wife
They've officially got a best friend for the rest of their life

And if one piece of advice they allowed me to say
I would say make sure that you cherish every hour of today
Because today as you celebrate as the new bride and groom
You two are the most special people here in this room

In every sight, every word every smell you must take pleasure,
As these are the things that for a lifetime you'll treasure,
So fill up your hearts with love from everyone and be proud,
Let the bells of the church celebrate your joy long and loud

And if you want the marriage to go the extra mile,
It helps each day that you wake up and wear a big smile.

Animal Antics

Cows are in the meadow,
Chewing on the grass.
They could be a little Frisian,
Like those monkeys made of brass

And whilst miners dug out black gold,
With which to warm our hearts,
The cows they churned out white gold
The cream to pour on tarts!

And when I talk of tarts,
I don't refer to mutton dressed as lamb,
I mean those little pastry cases,
Filled up to the brim with jam.

But if it's a sheep wearing a little pig face-mask
You'd have mutton dressed as ham!!

A very good friend of mine who sings with the Military Wives Choir
and who is the original girl with the leaky eyes!
Sarah Saunders

MILITARY WIVES

M	arried to the Forces
I	t's the Military Wives
L	inking Networks together
I	nspiring hope for each bride
T	houghts of one another
A	lways filling them with pride
R	ecalling sacrifices made
Y	ear upon year - the price that is paid

W	aking with thoughts of them each day they are gone
I	ndividually weak but together so strong
V	oicing yourselves in ways Gareth helps you sing
E	scaping to a place where music is king
S	inging in a choir - such support does it bring

SANDRINGHAM HOUSE

31st December 2015

Dear Mr. Griffiths,

    I am writing to thank you for your recent email and attachments which have been forwarded to me by Miss Rachel Wells.

    It was most kind of you to wish The Queen to see the photograph and also the poem, 'A Trip to London', which you were inspired to write, following your Investiture on 10th November 2015.

    Her Majesty was touched to hear of your pride and delight at receiving this award, and The Queen was so glad to know that you have been able to continue working for the Police despite being diagnosed with Parkinson's Disease at such a young age.

    I am to send you Her Majesty's best wishes for the coming year, and thank you once again for your thought in writing as you did.

Yours sincerely,

Susan Hussey.

Lady-in-Waiting

DC Hywel Griffiths, QPM

....and that children is why you should always eat your meat!!!

The Battle of Britain

These are my thoughts and what I have written,
As a tribute to those who fought in the Battle of Britain.
Heroes who fought for their country way up high,
Engaging in dog-fights where many would die.

And many of these warriors did indeed pay the price,
Willing to give their lives and make the ultimate sacrifice.
They did this because of their total faith and their trust,
That what they were doing was right and was just.

It is now 75 years since the Battle of Britain was fought,
And there are important lessons which should still be taught.
To make sure that the efforts of those young men so brave,
Are always remembered for the commitment they gave.

What was achieved was done in circumstances so dire,
With so much dependence placed on the brilliant Spitfire.
But how close to defeat we came, not many really knew,
...and never was so much owed by so many to so few.

With this famous partial quote from Winston Churchill,
The Battle epitomised the hope that victory did instil.
And even today as great threats to our nation we face,
In our armed forces the security of our nation we place.

**But the service they give – with danger is fraught,
And to be successful our Forces need our total support.**

The Defective Detective

That's me – I've done it, I've gone and I've been,
On my trip up to London to see Her Majesty the Queen,
A fantastic experience and one that I'll always remember;
The day we went to the Palace on that day in November.

Dressed up to the nines in my whistle and flute;
(I had to explain to my father that I was referring to my suit),
I felt very humble to meet and shake hands with the Queen,
And a prouder man you will rarely have seen.

Carrying an aura of extreme wisdom and power,
She bore the majesty and grace of the most delicate flower,
At first it was an experience that seemed quite surreal,
But after the presentation there was no doubt it was real.

And after the award I can't think of anything much neater,
Than being approached by a Welsh speaking Beefeater.
He from North Wales more commonly known as a Gog,
From the thriving metropolis of Blaenau Ffestiniog.

And to complete the day I'd certainly met my match,
As there is no greater sleuth than that played by Mr Cumberbatch,
Who plays Holmes the most fantastic Victorian detective –
Though I've built up a reputation as Gwent's greatest defective!

All in The Eyes

Look into my eyes,
Tell me what do you see,
Do they still sparkle?
Do they still remind you of me?

For the eyes tell a story,
They reflect all you have seen,
Recalling all you have done,
Remembering all you have been.

And if you switch things around,
And from the inside you look out,
Does looking at yourself in a mirror,
Fill you with trepidation and doubt.

If this is the case then,
This is where we must be strong,
Because we're all better than our illness,
And I know I'm not wrong.

Then if we fight back,
Put the sparkle back in our lives,
We'll be abler to confront,
Each new challenge that arrives.

...and we can all take heart,
Lifting our spirits to the skies,
Just by listening to the wisdom
Of one of life's most ordinary guys!

A Reality Check

It still makes me wince as if I'm wearing too tight a bra,
When I see people taking for granted just how lucky they are,
'cos if they'd seen me today they might have thought or have thunk,
Either he's having a laugh or else he's totally drunk.

Yes, although I haven't drunk alcohol for over 6 years,
At times when I'm walking it looks as if I've drunk at least that many beers,
And if when you wake, you feel that you've had enough of it all,
Just think of me each morning when I can just about crawl.

My speech is impaired and my writing is crap,
But I still manage to be an optimistic chap,
And if I can still do this and still go the extra mile,
Then the least that you can do – is stop whingeing...
... and SMILE

A Simple Poem

Sad poems, bad poems,
Some just slightly mad poems,
Lad poems, Dad poems,
Some to make you cry poems,
Most my wife wonders why poems.

Inverse, converse
Just go back a bit- reverse!
Diverse, the second verse,
Put it in to song verse
Happy to be me verse!
Then my wife says enough verse!

Just some words to pass the time,
Written so that the lines will rhyme,
Collected together in my own simple style,
With a simple message – just wear a smile.
Then – Remember my promise I once made to me:
Each day simply try to be the best you can be!

The Voice of Experience

I may be old fashioned and set in my ways,
But experience has helped me through many long days.
And after 30 years spent working for Her Majesty the Queen,
I want to share some views on the future and what's been.

So loud is the empty vessel that no secrets it can keep,
Quiet are those hallowed waters that run so calm and so deep,
Brash and boastful are those who say that they are the best,
Humble are the quiet ones who simply answer any test.

Bullying the method where some idiots show off their power,
Mocking and demeaning to cause their targets to cower.
Courageous are those who have a strength hidden inside,
To stand up to these bullies, who they will no longer abide.

Humility, and trust are two of the values I hold most dear,
And I will fight for them always, with no prejudice or fear.
Because these are the basics for a fulsome and successful life,
As well as respect for your partner as I am reminded by my wife!

Finally, I feel that I must comment on the attitude of 'No ifs or buts',
When trying to start a debate on the effect of Police budget cuts.
We have lost so much experience and skills over recent times,
That I consider it worthy enough to raise in one of my rhymes.

And I feel that I must warn all of those politicians so fine;
You're at risk of stretching and breaking that Thin Blue Line

Armed Forces Day

This poem is written, so that in my own little way,
I can pay tribute to our Forces, this Armed Forces Day.
Fighting for our freedom in far distant lands,
In jungles, in snow and in shifting desert sands;
Willing to sacrifice even with your own life;
Each one of you a hero in a world full of strife.

Fighting for freedom amongst all the grief,
Working together, strengthened by a common belief,
Belief that what you are doing is right,
Belief that the cause is really worth the fight,
Your professionalism is nothing less than we'd expect,
And being the best you have our total respect.

I'd like to say Thank-You from all in this land,
Proud of our forces currently fighting in the sand,
And whilst we may all be fighting our own little wars,
I have Parkinson's – there's no need for applause.
We all respect you, and from far away admire
The courage and resilience that you show under fire.

And for those who have fallen I have the deepest regret,
But if we value our freedom – then we will never forget.

Gareth and the All Stars

When Wogan asked "So who can we phone",
There were few could match young Gareth Malone.
A master of music, who can make choirs like angels sing,
And through children in need much relief can he bring.

Wogan persuaded him to take up the cause,
Admitting that there may be one or two flaws:
It appeared that the basses didn't turn up at the races
And the tenors were like an out of tune 'New Faces'

The sopranos were out of sync with the pianos
And with Jo Brand well we know anything goes.
But he found a star when Mel agreed to go solo,
Singing the song 'Wake me up before you go"

And I raise my hat to each of you who took part,
In support of the stories that pluck the strings of the heart.
And what a magnificent job done indeed,
In support of the great work done by Children in Need.

And Gareth you yourself should take pride,
In what you achieve and the entertainment you provide.

Box With The Fox

One was called Fox,
The other liked to box,
And both used to charm people with ease,
Then they both suffered the same fate,
Hearing the words, we all hate:
"I'm afraid you've got Parkinson's Disease".

But now here's the rub,
That though we are now in the same club,
This isn't the only common thing that we share.
You see none of us have given in,
And to this club you can add the big Yin,
And about our fellow sufferers we really do care.

And now that our secret is out,
There should be absolutely no doubt,
About why we try to help so many others,
Because by showing we can cope,
We can give much needed hope

'TWITCHETY' ME

I may twitch,
I may wriggle,
I may jiggle about,
As I squirm,
People giggle,
I just want to shout...

Stop staring,
Start caring,
It's me can't you see
Still hurting,
Still wondering,
Why you're all staring at me!

I don't feel ill,
I just can't keep still,
It doesn't hurt not one little bit;
So I look on the bright side,
And I'll always keep smiling,
All this movement keeps me exceedingly fit.

ALWAYS SMILING

The Equaliser

Are the odds stacked against you, are you struggling to cope?
Do you need some help – do you need some hope,
Well if you're struggling to deal with vermin control,
Look no further than Baz and his rat-catching patrol.

Famous as a police officer, enticing crook to jump in his car,
And often afterwards found retelling his story in a bar.
Whilst the nemesis of the miners was old Mrs Thatcher,
The rats feel the same about Baz the 'Rat Catcher'.

And Baz found that enjoyment in work was refired,
Not long after he had left the police force and retired.
But policing and catching the rats are very much the same,
You both try and outwit each other – it's only a game

So if you want help to get rid of the pests in your lives,
(Those little furry ones - he wouldn't dream of taking on wives,)
Then either just text him – or give him a call,
You'll get rid of the vermin, and you'll also have a ball!

The Choir-Master

He's back he's here - it's Gareth MALLONE
The. thinking man's answer to Sylvester Stallone.
Trying to organise a reunion of his choral groups
Including the school and the wives of the troops.
Gareth began at the school and by playing his Trump Card
He earned the respect of The Rappers on the schoolyard.
Imran showed the rewards of respect - and answered the call,
When he sang the solo for his school at the Albert Hal
After the school Gareth took up the challenge of South Oxon,
and with Dee the soloist he found someone to count on.
He brought life into a town that had seemed quite run down,
To show if you give life to the community you give life to the town.
I think his finest and most moving collaboration of them all,
Was his work with the military wives and their partners one and all.
I have written many poems and praised these ladies to the skies.
Being rewarded by my friendship with the girl who has leaky eyes
Gareth is inspirational and has a unique edge to his manner
which makes all members proud to sing under his banner
and he has shown how music can have a positive impact on lives.
something admirably shown by those military wives
I have written this poem intending to write about all from the start,
but watching the wives so brave has struck a chord in my heart;
Gareth in the future you know whatever you do and where ever you are
you have left such precious memories that friends will never be far.
Gareth – you Sir are a Legend and an inspiration to all,
And I would personally like to Thank-You for the fantastic
Entertainment you have given to us over many years.

With a special Thanks to Sarah SAUNDERS
and her husband who she supports as a military wife,

KEEP SMILING

46

Mark Sutton – A Detective's Detective

This tribute is to you Sir – possibly Gwent's Greatest Detective,
From one you showed faith in- even though I'm defective!
Not mentally though - now that would be silly,
The one you mean there is that mad Irishman WILLY!

Yes, we worked as a team once in Ebbw Vale Upper,
To catch a little tinker during Operation Scupper.
They all looked the same, and they all were called Jimmy
Apart from the sister who I think they called Timmy

With your trusty Lieutenant, Mr. Davies – that's Glyn,
Ebbw Vale's own answer to Stacey's nice Uncle Bryn.
You led us and took us to places so near and so far,
Always seeming to end up close to a pub or a bar.

And it was on one of these trips to The Smoke,
That a top gipsy fighter met a more dangerous bloke...
Said Sonny "I'm the hardest in Britain – King of the Plot"
Said Martin from Merthyr "On that point you're NOT!"

But before these two beasts did each other some harm,
Willie smarmed in with sweet Irish charm.
And in his own way he hit the nail on the button,
Saying "You don't want to upset me old Mr SUTTON"

We built up some friendships in those many years past,
Formed largely by you and the net that you cast.
Take Kerry and Tiger - each day in Smiths they did look
And that's the only time Kerry has ever finished a book

Times now have changed and you've put on graces and airs,
And I'm writing poems like Caerphilly's Pam Ayres,
But the reason I write this and say it I must,
Is that between us together we had absolute trust.

It's been an honour to know you, and call you a friend,
Although sometimes we drove you right round the bend,
And beneath that exterior so hard and so cold,
We know there beats a heart, made from solid gold.

Thanks from an old dog handler

Ken I write this recalling a dark stormy night,
When you came to my rescue and saved me my sight.
It all began on a cold night at a petrol station in Cwmbran;
My dog was no help because he was locked in the van.

I had simply asked a drunk to be quiet and move along,
He replied "I'm going nowhere – you've got that all f**king wrong"
When he appeared at court he would say it was only a cough;
But I heard him say clearly – "The magistrates are all tw*ts
...and you can f**k off"

I had no other choice than arrest him but he soon cut up rough,
And I couldn't quite work out how a drunk could be so tough.
Though it became obvious when he started to gouge out my eyes -
That this drunk was a paratrooper trained to fall from the skies.

But luckily help came – though not one who was much of a looker,
The best part was that - he used to play for Wales as a hooker.
And though to escape - this drunk would go to any length
He was no match for Ken's a legendary tower of strength!

Justin – 'OH GOOD GRIEF'!

A Tribute to the Legend that is Justin O'KEEFFE

I have over 30 years of service in the police –
If convicted of murder – I could apply for release.
But some of the best moments as strange as it may seem
Were when working with Justin on Gwent's Major Incident team!

For this legend of mine who is so much fun,
Has now reached the tender age of half a ton.
And the king of Grecian 2000 can oft be heard say;
I don't know what all the fuss is about 50 shades of grey!

A great family man he lives for his boys,
Though I can imagine Justin playing with all of their toys.
I've met him at cross country races run in the freezing cold,
Where through his support he reveals his heart of pure gold.

My favourite description of him is that he is fiercely loyal;
And his support for me has certainly made me feel like a royal.
Justin is the sort of leader you would follow to the bitter end;
And Justin it's been an honour to work with you – but more-so
...to call you a friend!

Now –Let's get this party started!

Feelings

I wish I could be more open,
Telling people how I really feel,
I may not always show it,
But my feelings are for real.

I rarely tell my Mum and Dad,
That I love them very much.
It's something that I've never done,
I'm not blessed with the Gentle Touch.

But deep within is a sensitive side –
Which I very rarely show.
A gentle and a caring man,
Only shown to those I really know.

I have very deep profound beliefs,
Which help me live my life and cope,
And whatever challenges face me,
I face them with optimism and with hope.

Backed up by the promise
I once made from me to me,
I'll face whatever life deals out,
By striving to be **'The Best That I Can Be!**

In a City

In a city,
Inner city,
Down town,
Down turn
Less jobs,
Less we earn.
What hope for the Working Man?
What hope for the Greater Plan?

Less homes,
More homeless,
Building desire,
Fuelling need,
Fuelled by
Corporate greed.
Is there still a Working Man?
Who's in charge of the Greater Plan?

Global terror,
Global war,
No longer sure,
What the fight is for,
The Global Terrorist,
Now lives next door.
Fanfare for the Common Man
With whom we trust the Greater Plan.

And fight we must,
One and all,
Standing fast,
Standing tall.
We cannot fail,
Lest all will fall.
The Working and the Common Man,
Stand together and defeat all we can!

Parkinson's is Permanent

Parkinson's is permanent,
You cannot cure it with a knife,
So if diagnosed, you must accept:
It's now with you for the rest of your life.

If you just accept this fact;
Then very swiftly move along,
You can prove to all of those doubters,
That you can cope, and all of them are wrong.

I won't pretend it's easy,
And daily challenges you will face,
Simply try to do the best you can
And the joys of life you can still embrace.

You're better than this disease,
And I will prove it if I can,
Still working after seventeen years,
I'm proud to call myself a 'Lucky Man!'

Thoughts of an Ex Dog Handler

I've worked with many fine people, in many different places,
But sometimes I have difficulty putting names to the faces.
You see as a dog handler – I was one of the few,
And though I didn't know them – of me most cops knew.

And even now, seventeen years after leaving the dogs,
I'm still often reminded of some memorable logs.
Many police officers still remember me as the dog man;
With Jacko primed to attack as soon as he got out of the van.

There was the memorable incident with Mike Williams in Cwmbran Town,
When instead of disarming a man from a hammer – his dog 'PACE' just sat down,
Well 'PACE' became 'PEACE' and losing our reputation, the most serious of matters.
Rescued by Jacko who ripped the armed man's legs into tatters.

My times on the Dog Section were some of the best of my life,
And the dog became part of the family with my kids and my wife,
I was never the best dog handler, following Jacko at a fast jog
But I WAS one of the best police officers to be trained with a dog.

There's nothing quite like tracking down a burglar who's broken into a house,
Though I've had a similar buzz by detecting crime with my mouse!

Remembrance Today
(DIY SOS)

These are my thoughts told in my own humble way –
A tribute to our Armed Forces this Remembrance Day.
Sometimes it's difficult knowing how or where to start,
But my feelings are real and from the bottom of my heart.

People suffering because of sacrifices once made,
It is our duty to ensure that in all ways they are repaid.
Soldiers badly wounded as for our safety they did serve,
Needing help to rehabilitate – the least that they deserve.

They paid the cost of fighting for their country when at war,
We must show them that the cause was well worth fighting for.
So many limbs lost, and so much mental damage caused,
Now it is our duty that their traumas are at least paused.

And to those yobs who to the wounded are so unkind,
It would be nice to see the SAS creep up on them from behind.
Then teach this group of social misfits the value of respect,
And show them the dignity - the least our heroes should expect.

This poem is also my way of saying Thank-You DIY SOS;
For creating homes from such a complete and utter mess.
You've shown everyone what a positive approach can achieve,
If we all work together and if we all together believe.

And one final tribute to the Prince of Darkness (Young Willy)
Royally named by the one and only (and not so young) Billy.

A Champion for the Disabled

I've got a friend who's very special to me,
He can't hear very well and he can't really see,
But if you're looking for a role model or just inspiration,
There is surely no better in the whole of our nation.

I thank that the reason that we get on so well,
Is that he can barely understand any word I do tell.
And although he appears so confident and strong,
He worries people may think there's nothing wrong.

He faces great challenges just to get through each day
He does this with no complaining always saying he's O.K.
I know that he will cope – that's the mark of the man,
Blessed with his young son and the delightful Leanne.

Jeremey is a legend and a champion for the disabled,
Working harder than most of even those who are abled.
And from a man who promises to always be the best I can be:
I can't thank-you enough for being a daily inspiration to me!

"Boom. Really? Please."

Bearing a burden, many would struggle to carry,
This poem starts out as a tribute to Prince Harry.
It's the story of royalty, of an heir to the throne,
And what he achieves with young Gareth Malone.

Providing support for the Invictus games,
Now followed by Obama and other big names.
Harry and Gary showed what you can actually do,
If you believe in people and let them believe in you.

Because after a start with some difficult choices,
The ones who they chose now sing with melodious voices,
And this choir Invictus made up from troops injured at war,
Makes me feel humbled and of their achievements in awe

So let us not have doubts, let us not dither or Tarry,
Cry freedom for Gary and his matey Prince Harry.
And just as America tried to 'Up the Ante' by a few degrees,
The Queen swiftly re-butted them with
        "Boom. Really? Please."

Why Me?

(A question I never ask about having Parkinson's disease)

Y o why, oh me - oh my -Time flies
Why are there so many X's and so, many Y's?
And why can Y sound like a question itself
Or is it a play upon words from the xxx top-shelf.

Because X on its own can mean something else instead,
Like something that's censored and shouldn't be read.
But put these together and I hope you can see,
How I've censored myself to never ask me "Why Me?"

It's my way of coping with a disease so unfair,
That it makes people laugh and it makes people stare.
It's hard when they poke fun because of the way that I walk,
And I can't always answer them because I can't always talk.

I talk about my problems through the medium of rhyme,
So I can make people aware this abuse is actually a crime.
And back to the question why do I never ask me "Why Me?"
Because I've got it – I just get on with it – as it always shall be.

And by facing daily challenges with a smile on my face,
I can keep "Why Me?" locked up in a very secure place.

Cry For P.T.S.D.

(Post-Traumatic Stress Disorder) P.T.S.D.

Pulling the shutters down,
A forgotten past – a derelict town,
A description of post-traumatic stress disorder,
A soldier cursed for life for simply following an order.

It's hard to imagine the torture you might find,
If you could read the thoughts of each troubled mind.
...and yet so many of our past soldiers, so humble and brave,
Suffer so badly that they seek the comfort of an early grave.

This doesn't seem right – it doesn't seem fair,
But why should we worry – why should we care?
Simply because these heroes are willing to give up their lives,
Fighting for their Queen, Country and military wives.

Yes, these fantastic ladies who give so much support,
Hoping for a safe return after dangerous battles have been fought.
And the efforts of the Military Choirs and their sweet angelic voices,
Leave little doubt that we must face up to some very difficult choices.

Either ignore the suffering and simply bury our heads deep down in the sand,
OR accept the debt that we owe to those who fight for the security of our land.
So please just take a minute – think, then sing their praises to the sky.
As Lulu shown her support with the release of her latest single called 'CRY'!

You might like other Poetry books by Hywel Griffiths.

Published by Cambria Books.

Poems, Parkinson's, the Police and Me

ISBN: 978-0-9928690-6-9

POEMS,
PARKINSON'S,
the POLICE
and ME

Reflections of my life told in verse
PC Hywel Griffiths

POEMS,
PARKINSON'S,
and
THE BEST I CAN BE

A further collection of poems written
to make you smile, cry, laugh or think!
(or any combination of these!)
Hywel Griffiths QPM, BSc.

Poems, Parkinson's and the best I can be

ISBN: 978-0-9933567-5-9

www.ingramcontent.com/pod-product-compliance
Lightning Source LLC
Chambersburg PA
CBHW071635040426
42452CB00009B/1630